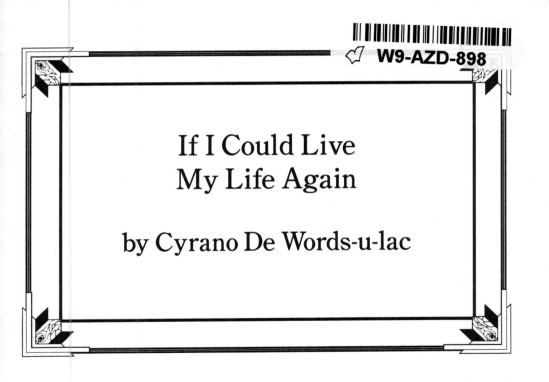

If I Could Live My Life Again

by Cyrano De Words-u-lac

If I Could Live My Life Again
ISBN 1-56292-050-2
Copyright © 1996 Dan and Dave Davidson
Rhymeo Ink
P.O. Box 1416
Salem, Virginia 24153

Application has been made for a registered federal trademark for "Rhymeo" and "Show-It Poet."

Published by Honor Books
P.O. Box 55325
Tulsa, Oklahoma 74155

WHAT'S A RHYMEO™?

Rhymeos™ are fat-free un-poetry lite and lean literary cuisine. Rhymeos™ are short and sketchy, quick and catchy—two short lines reinforced in rhyme. Although the short rhyming couplets display a poetic flavor, they are not traditional poetry. They are actually jingles about life Jingle—Verse Poetry for the 21st Century—offering insight and motivation, humor and inspiration.

Cyrano De Words-u-lac pens the shortest verse in the universe—a story to tell in a nutshell, a rhyming report to make a long story short. Rhymeos™ are short and sweet and poetically petite—clever ways to paraphrase—bite-sized words to the wise. Whether concise advice or an easy doesy fuzzy wuzzy, Rhymeos™ give a reflective perspective in a fireside chat format. It's literary rap with a snap—poetically correct dialect—a way to cope with humor and hope!

Life Story Inventory
Picture yourself sitting on a rocking chair in the shade,
with writing pen and paper, sipping lemonade.

Look Ahead
Imagine your last days on earth
measure in your mind your life's worth.

Write Down Each Wish
Replay your life, record, and reflect
each wish, dream, reward, and regret.

Send It Back In Time
Take the memo in your mind
and send it back in time.

Live The List
Begin to live your life the way
you'd live it again, starting today.

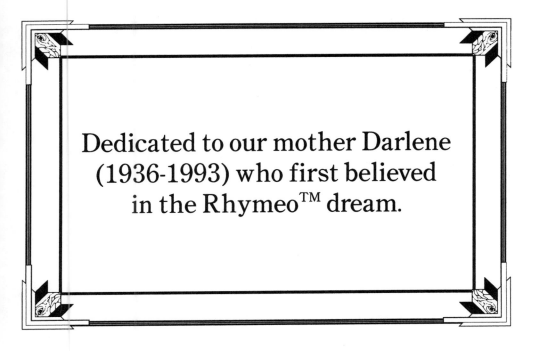

Dedicated to our mother Darlene
(1936-1993) who first believed
in the Rhymeo™ dream.

I'd vow
to do it now.

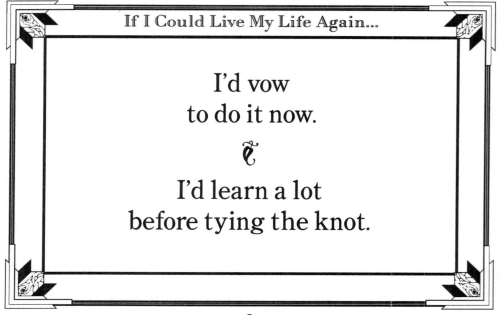

I'd learn a lot
before tying the knot.

I'd live each day under the sun as if it might be my last one.

I'd send more regards
with chocolates and cards.

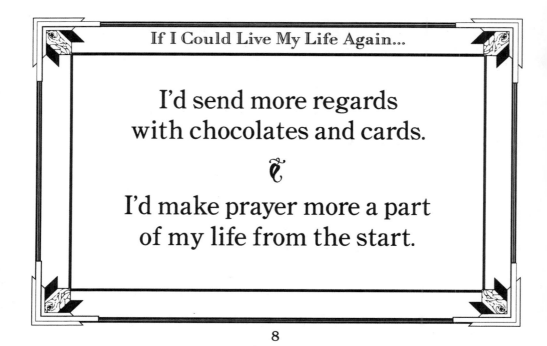

I'd make prayer more a part
of my life from the start.

I'd put my spouse first,
for better or worse.

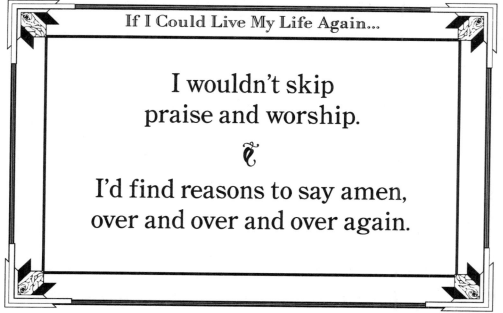

I wouldn't skip
praise and worship.

I'd find reasons to say amen,
over and over and over again.

I'd lay up treasure
in heavenly measure.

Each day I'd do my best,
up until the time to rest.

C

I'd fill my life with laughter
happily ever after.

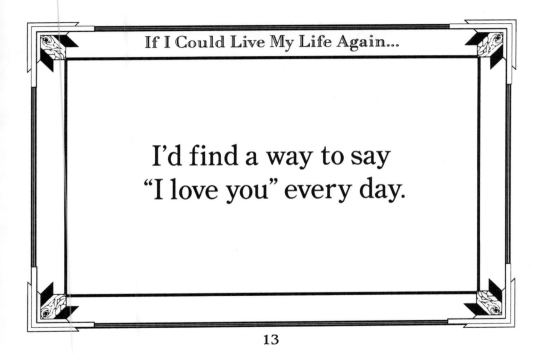

I'd find a way to say
"I love you" every day.

In times of emergency,
I'd have a sense of urgency.

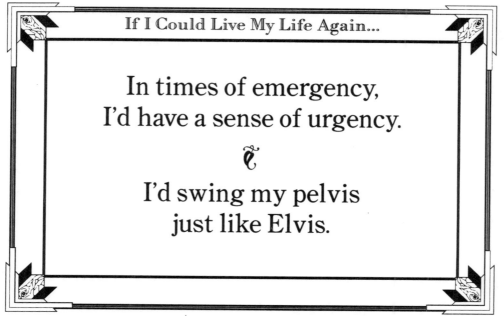

I'd swing my pelvis
just like Elvis.

I'd ask what I could do
for the red, white, and blue.

I'd plant more flowers
and work less hours.

I'd volunteer to coach a team
for my child's self-esteem.

I'd keep my word
how it was heard.

I'd never miss
a good-bye kiss.

I'd avoid traitors
and alligators.

I'd dance and twirl
with my little girl.

I wouldn't judge by race,
nor by the color of a face.

*

I wouldn't gossip or gab,
rattle, tattle, blurt, or blab.

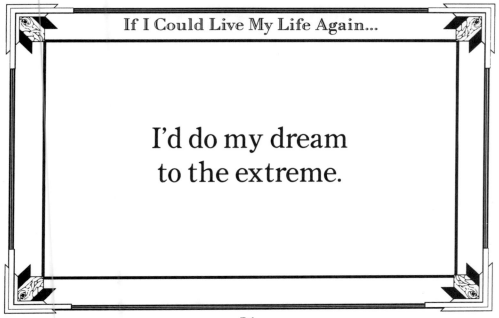

I'd do my dream
to the extreme.

I'd hold my honey's hand
and write love notes in the sand.

My life would be slower;
I'd be less of a goer.

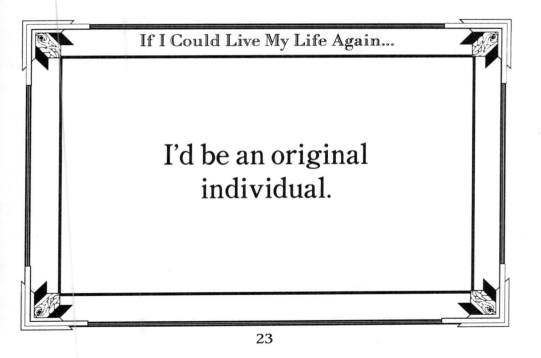

If I Could Live My Life Again...

I'd be an original
individual.

I'd be a witness
for health and fitness.

℃

I'd believe in the reason
for the Christmas season.

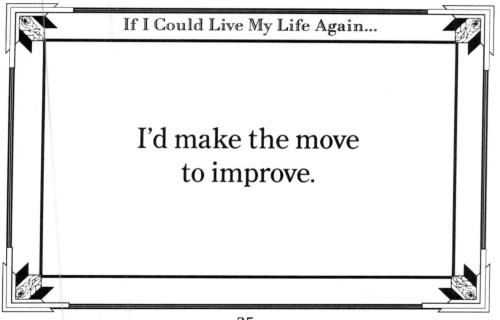

I'd make the move
to improve.

I'd be a solution
for reducing pollution.

I'd never dilly-dally
in a dark alley.

At the county fair,
I'd win a stuffed bear.

Lovey dovey I would allow,
but hanky panky only with a vow.

C

I'd give more God bless you's
after impromptu achoo's.

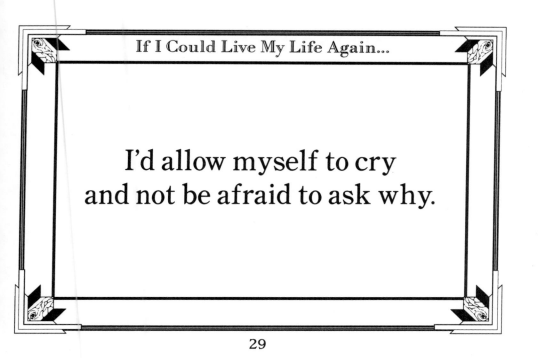

I'd allow myself to cry
and not be afraid to ask why.

Guilt in my heart I'd forego,
when taste testing cookie dough.

More cookies I'd dunk
in milk ... kerplunk.

I'd never choose
to falsely accuse.

I'd say all there is to be said,
before a loved one's death bed.

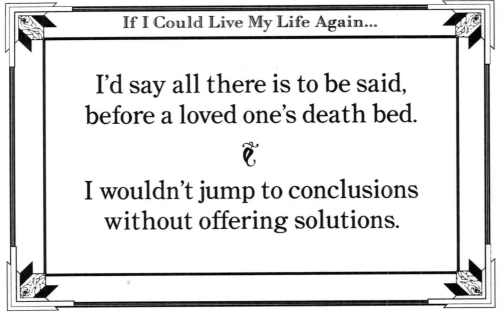

I wouldn't jump to conclusions
without offering solutions.

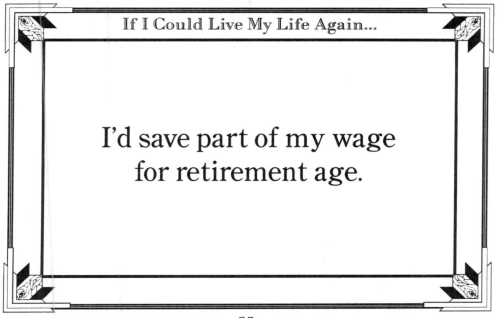

If I Could Live My Life Again...

I'd save part of my wage
for retirement age.

I wouldn't let
my heart regret.

I'd develop a thirst
for first things first.

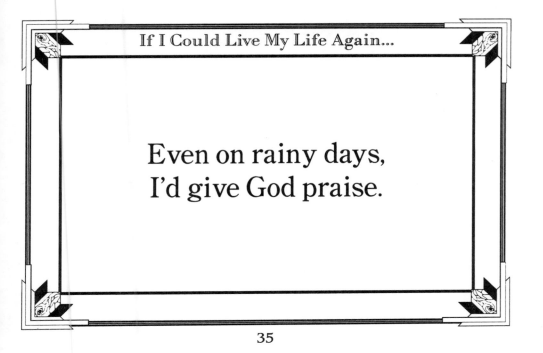

Even on rainy days,
I'd give God praise.

I wouldn't use alibis
when it came to exercise.

C

Sometimes I'd choose
to oversnooze.

I'd sing a lullaby
when babies cry.

I'd try to mingle
more as a single.

I'd avoid the snare
of having an affair.

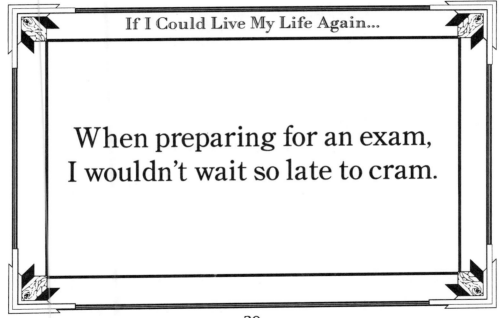

When preparing for an exam,
I wouldn't wait so late to cram.

I'd be more reflective
on goals and objectives.

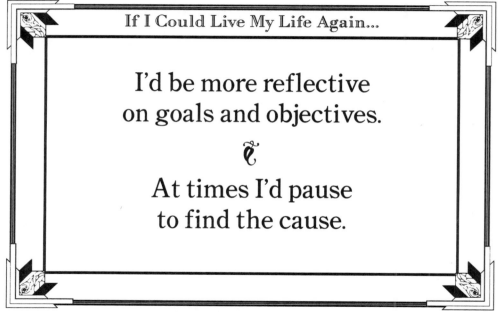

At times I'd pause
to find the cause.

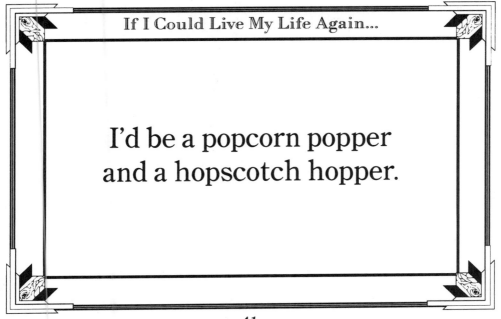

I'd be a popcorn popper
and a hopscotch hopper.

I'd carry a camera on trips
to capture creative clips.

❦

I'd realize failure from before
was opportunity at my door.

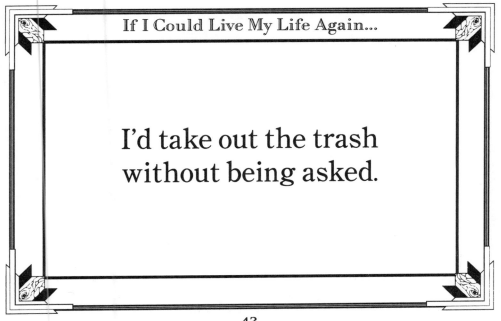

I'd take out the trash
without being asked.

Never in vain,
would I take God's name.

I wouldn't mind the hassle
of a graduation tassel.

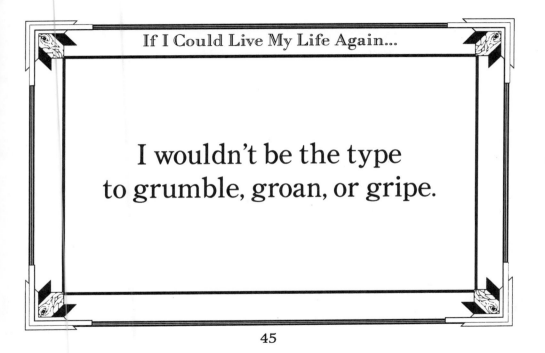

I wouldn't be the type
to grumble, groan, or gripe.

Class reunions I'd attend
to reminisce with old friends.

I'd have more pillow fights
on slumber party nights.

I'd be a hula-hooper,
not a party pooper.

Daily I'd design
ways to streamline.

🍂

I'd witness and share
in word, deed, and prayer.

I'd thank those who
fought before, defending
our country in war.

I'd never fall
for the crystal ball.

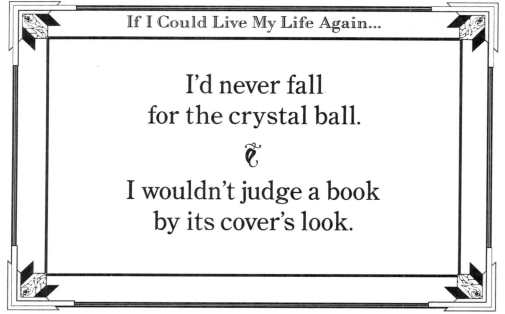

I wouldn't judge a book
by its cover's look.

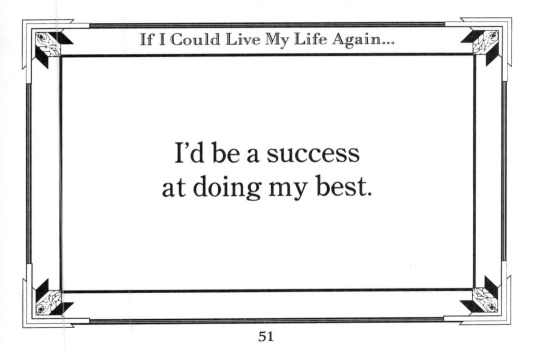

I'd be a success
at doing my best.

At video return time,
I'd be kind and rewind.

C

I'd be a quicker wiper
of a dirty diaper.

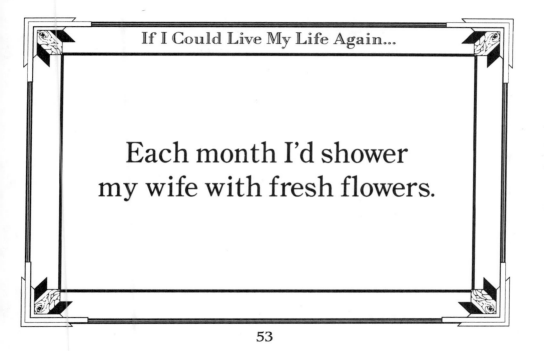

Each month I'd shower
my wife with fresh flowers.

Rather than sit on the fence,
I'd take stands with confidence.

I wouldn't let the sun go down
if anger was still around.

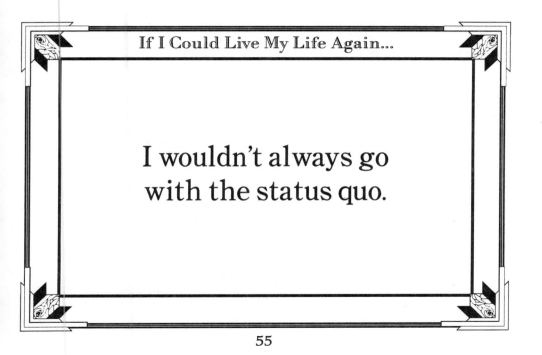

I wouldn't always go
with the status quo.

With Grandpa I'd spend more time,
feeding pigeons in parks to unwind.

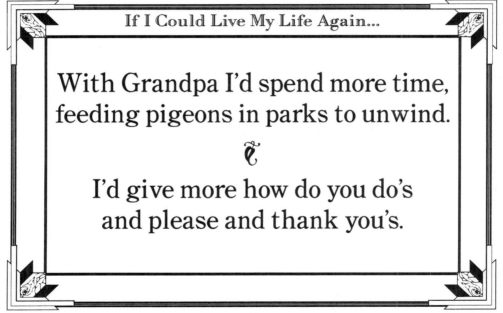

I'd give more how do you do's
and please and thank you's.

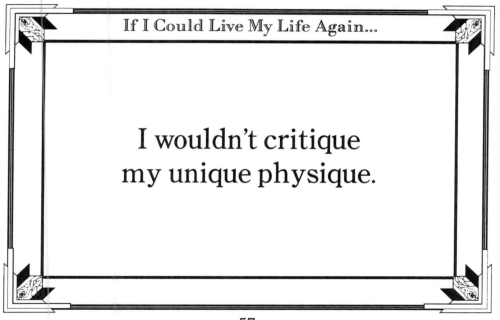

If I Could Live My Life Again...

I wouldn't critique
my unique physique.

With my dog and cat,
I'd dialog and chit-chat.

I'd surrender my heavy load
and walk the narrow road.

I'd give relief
to those in grief.

I'd buy less stuff;
enough is enough.

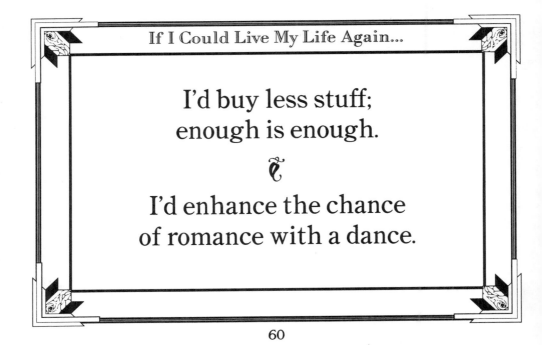

I'd enhance the chance
of romance with a dance.

I'd use coupons more
at the grocery store.

I'd avoid one night stands
and keep it to shaking hands.

I'd avoid the grief
of being a thief.

If I Could Live My Life Again...

I wouldn't complain
in the check out lane.

I'd fill out my will
before I became ill.

&

I'd add perspiration
to my inspiration.

I'd be sure my spine
stayed in line.

Instead of a divorce,
I'd try to stay the course.

❦

My sweetie I'd swoon
under the moon.

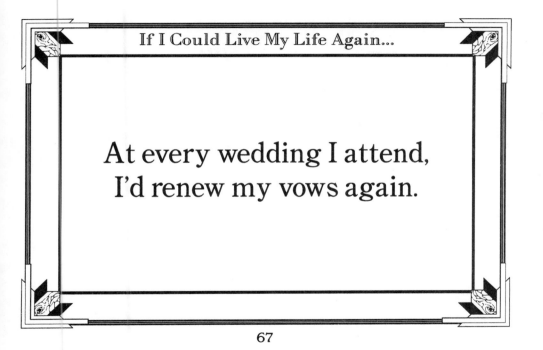

At every wedding I attend,
I'd renew my vows again.

My self pity
would be itty-bitty.

ટ્

I'd stretch for perfection
in my chosen direction.

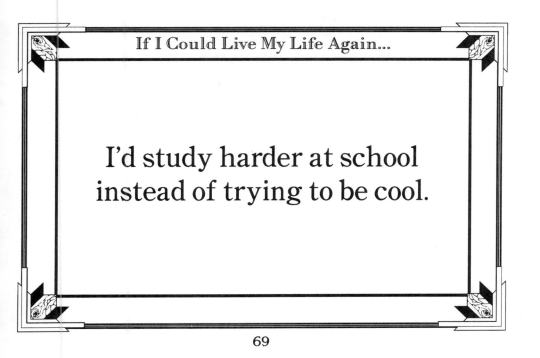

I'd study harder at school
instead of trying to be cool.

At times I'd be blunt
when I need to confront.

I'd send thank you notes
with heartfelt quotes.

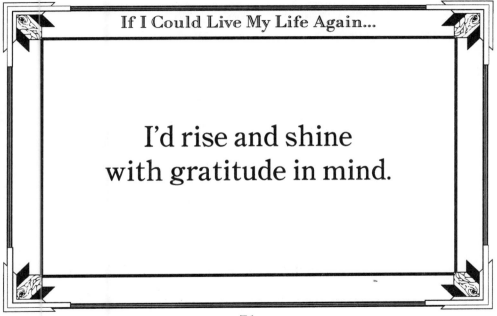

I'd rise and shine
with gratitude in mind.

I'd learn to understand
the language of another land.

❧

I wouldn't count on luck
to ever make a buck.

If I saw prints from reindeer paws, I'd wonder about Santa Claus.

I'd avoid the bottle
when pushing the throttle.

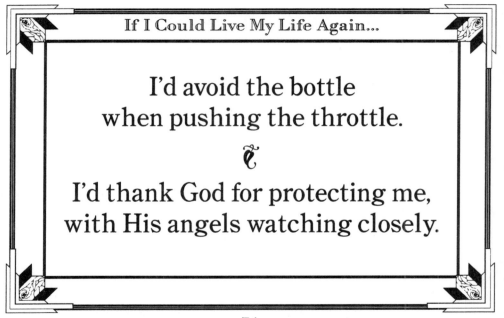

I'd thank God for protecting me,
with His angels watching closely.

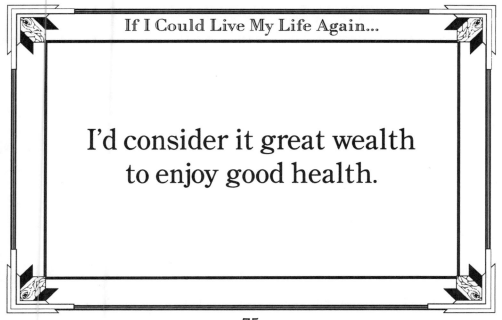

If I Could Live My Life Again...

I'd consider it great wealth
to enjoy good health.

I'd do more brainstorming
and creative idea forming.

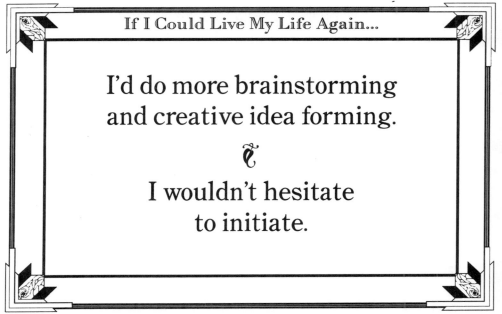

I wouldn't hesitate
to initiate.

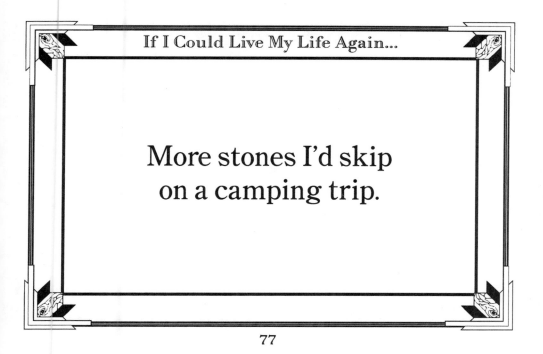

More stones I'd skip
on a camping trip.

I'd get a tutor
for my computer.

❦

I wouldn't be late
or procrastinate.

I wouldn't devote my soul
to the remote control.

I'd overlook a flaw
in my mother-in-law.

When my room's a disaster,
I'd clean it up faster.

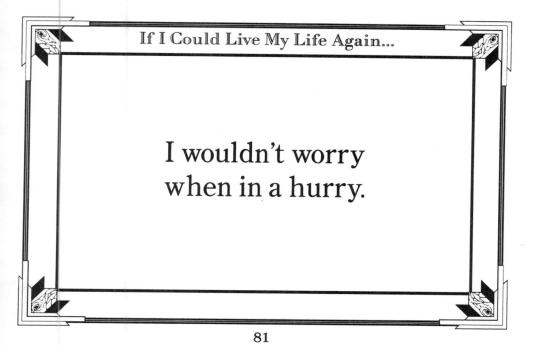

If I Could Live My Life Again...

I wouldn't worry
when in a hurry.

81

I'd have the wisdom
for a backup system.

*

I wouldn't devise
little white lies.

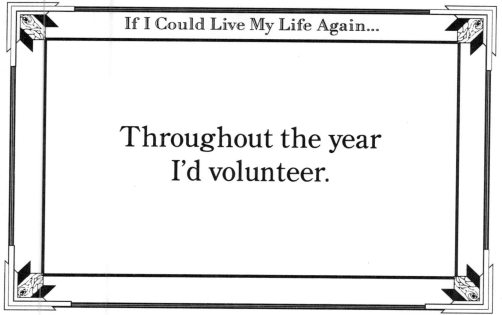

Throughout the year
I'd volunteer.

I'd take my chances
on career advances.

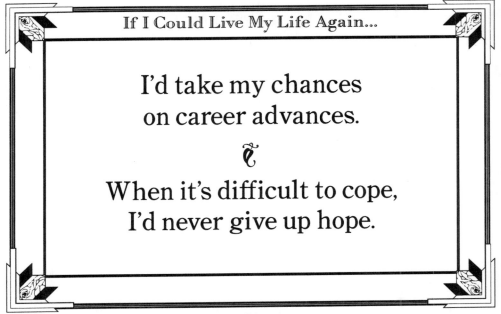

When it's difficult to cope,
I'd never give up hope.

If I Could Live My Life Again...

I'd put more pep
in my step.

I'd give a good tip,
not a stiff upper lip.

I'd be a good loser,
not an excuser.

I'd give more
to the poor.

For the safety of all,
smoke detectors I'd install.

I wouldn't make fun
of anyone.

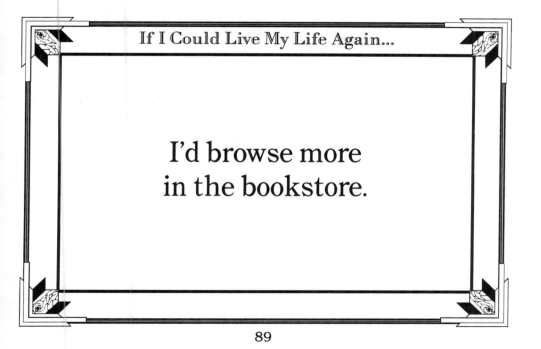

If I Could Live My Life Again...

I'd browse more
in the bookstore.

I'd make a pledge
to support an orphanage.

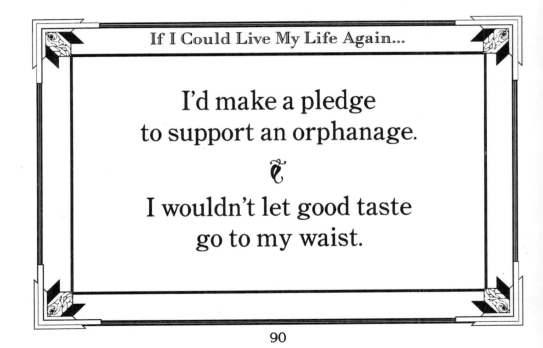

I wouldn't let good taste
go to my waist.

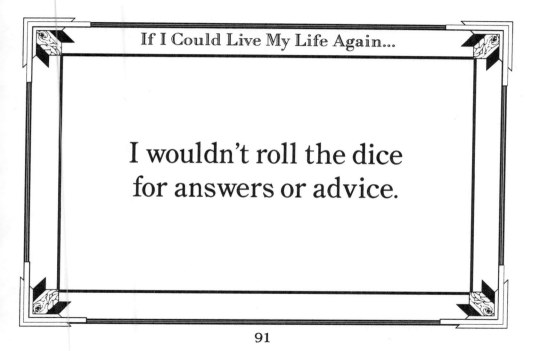

I wouldn't roll the dice
for answers or advice.

I'd proudly salute
a military recruit.

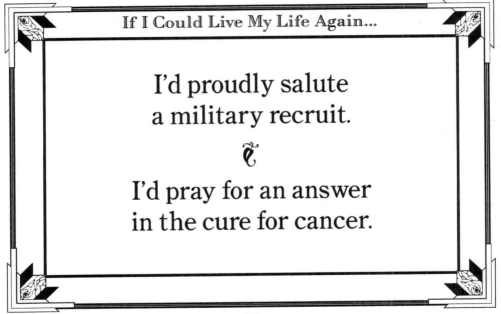

I'd pray for an answer
in the cure for cancer.

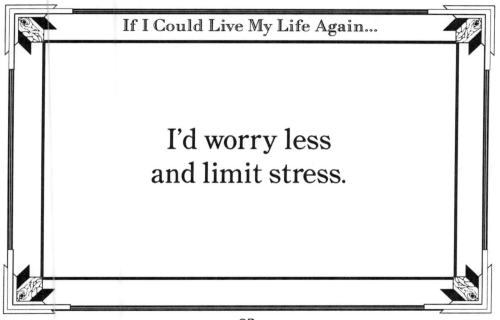

If I Could Live My Life Again...

I'd worry less
and limit stress.

I wouldn't will
to hate or kill.

I'd take time to greet
people on the street.

"Wolf" I wouldn't cry,
nor would I try to lie.

I'd build my house on land
filled with rock instead of sand.

I'd be more of a crusader
than a sideline spectator.

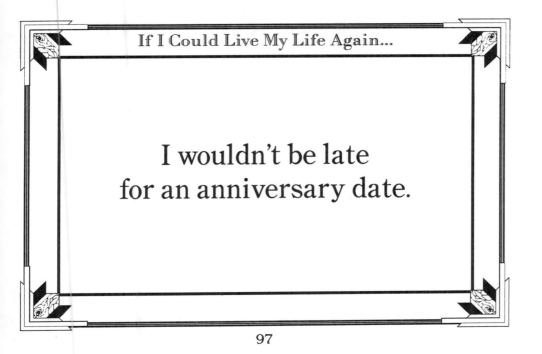

I wouldn't be late
for an anniversary date.

When feeling all alone,
I'd leave my comfort zone.

❦

I wouldn't camp
without a lamp.

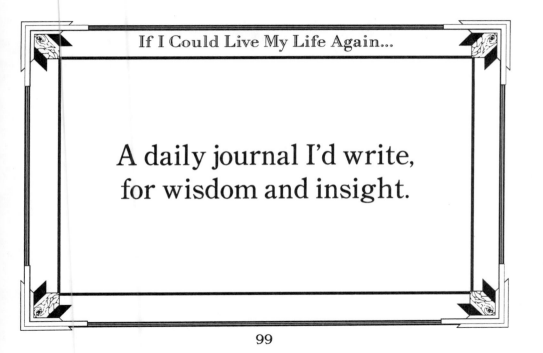

If I Could Live My Life Again...

A daily journal I'd write,
for wisdom and insight.

I would invest
in what stood the test.

I'd serve breakfast in bed
to my newlywed.

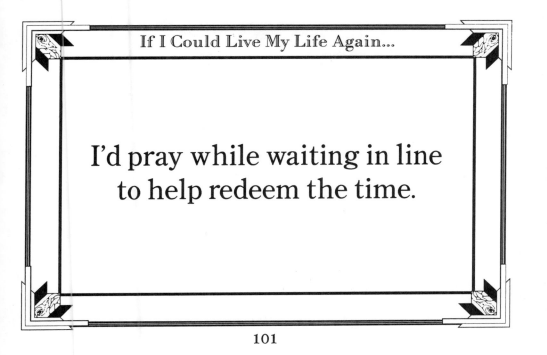

I'd pray while waiting in line
to help redeem the time.

Out on the court
I'd be a good sport.

I'd avoid the thorn
of porn.

If I Could Live My Life Again...

I'd appreciate more art
like Monet and Mozart.

Even if my boss was rude,
I'd work with a good attitude.

C

I wouldn't make excuses with
"if only" and "what if."

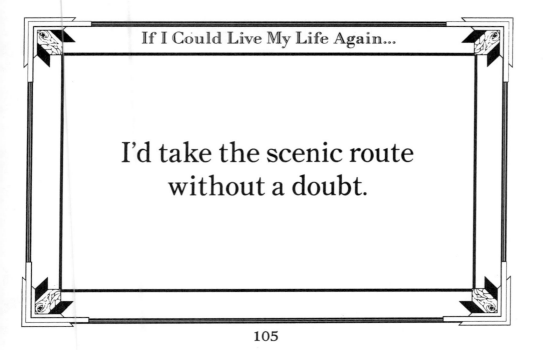

I'd take the scenic route
without a doubt.

As a campfire host,
more marshmallows I'd roast.

I'd give gifts with Christmas bows
and kiss lips under mistletoes.

I'd make it a must
to have more trust.

Once a week I'd relax
and tune out what distracts.

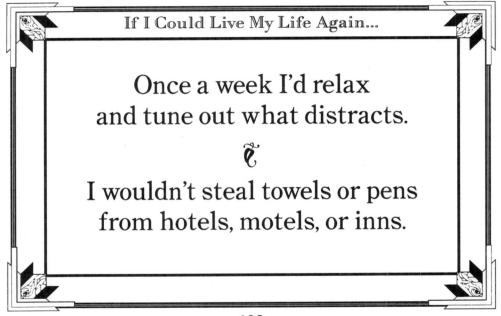

I wouldn't steal towels or pens
from hotels, motels, or inns.

I'd be a trail blazer
and a people praiser.

With a clean slate,
I'd forgive my mate.

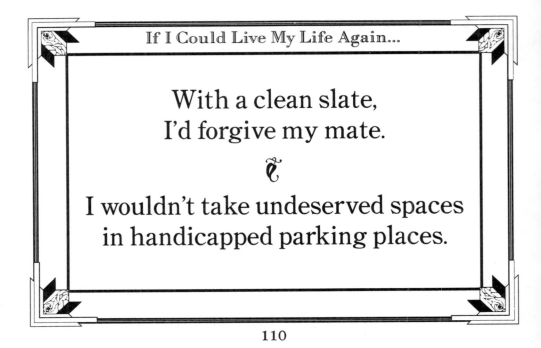

I wouldn't take undeserved spaces
in handicapped parking places.

Life I'd choose
over the blues.

I'd repair a bad hair day
with mousse and hair spray.

℃

I'd write down Grandma's recipes
and ask about our family tree.

If I Could Live My Life Again...

I'd keep in mind
the finish line.

I'd be content
and quick to repent.

I wouldn't waver
in doing a favor.

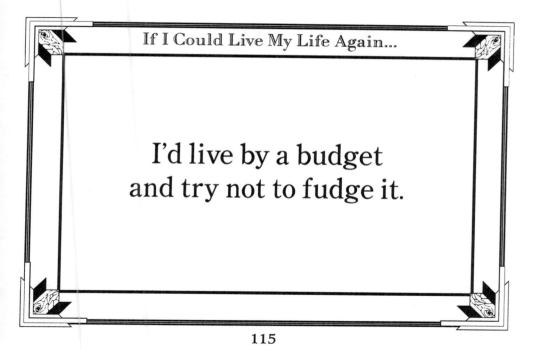

I'd live by a budget
and try not to fudge it.

No matter where I roam,
I'd cherish home sweet home.

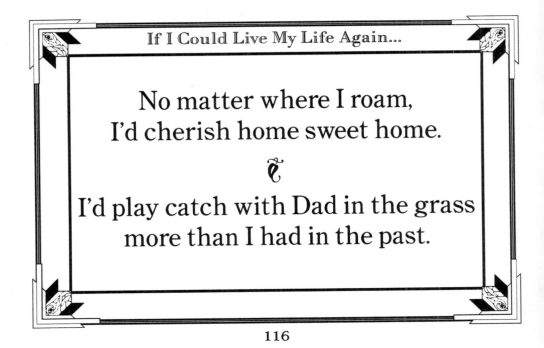

I'd play catch with Dad in the grass
more than I had in the past.

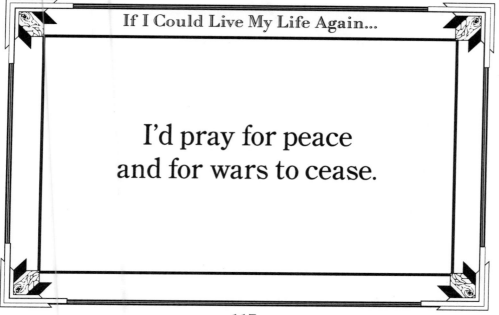

If I Could Live My Life Again...

I'd pray for peace
and for wars to cease.

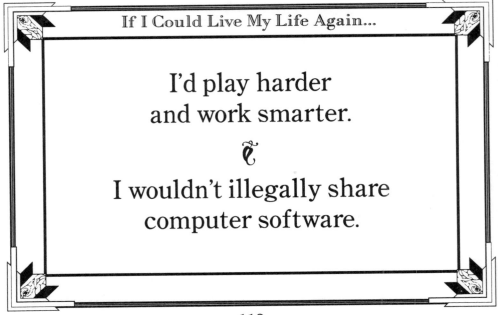

I'd play harder
and work smarter.

I wouldn't illegally share
computer software.

I'd be one in which to confide
for others hurting deep inside.

I'd repeat less rumor
and spread more humor.

I'd do whatever it took to find
with God a daily quiet time.

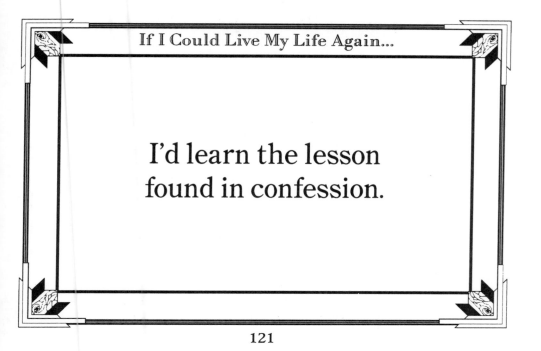

I'd learn the lesson
found in confession.

I'd follow a plan
of fiber and bran.

I'd coordinate my wardrobe
from shoelace to earlobe.

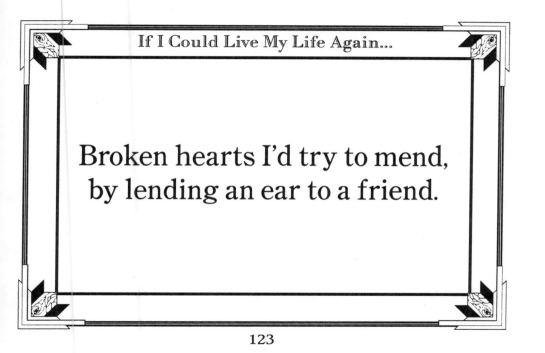

Broken hearts I'd try to mend,
by lending an ear to a friend.

I'd be a pioneer
and open a frontier.

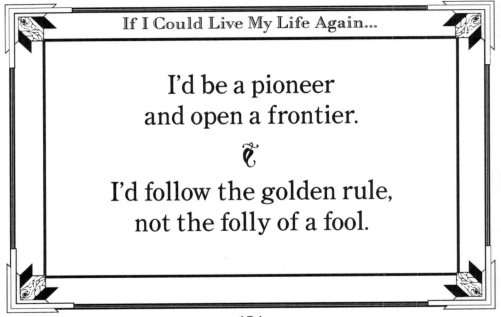

I'd follow the golden rule,
not the folly of a fool.

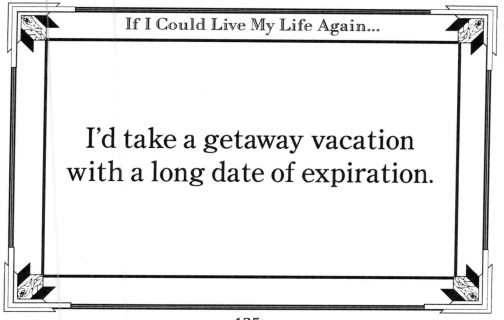

I'd take a getaway vacation
with a long date of expiration.

I'd be less courageous
around germs contagious.

If two roads from one unraveled,
I'd choose the one less traveled.

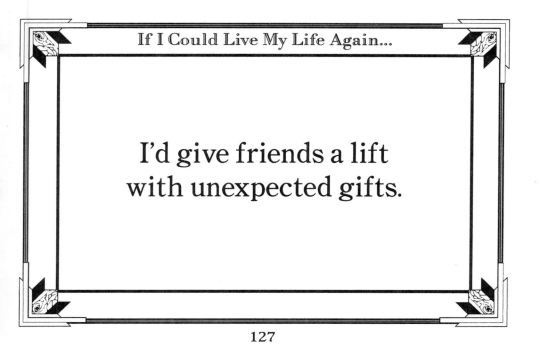

I'd give friends a lift
with unexpected gifts.

I'd give up horoscopes
and operas from the soaps.

My new year's resolution
would be a revolution.

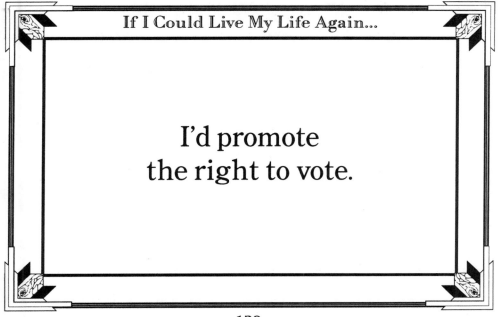

I'd promote
the right to vote.

I'd be bolder
as I got older.

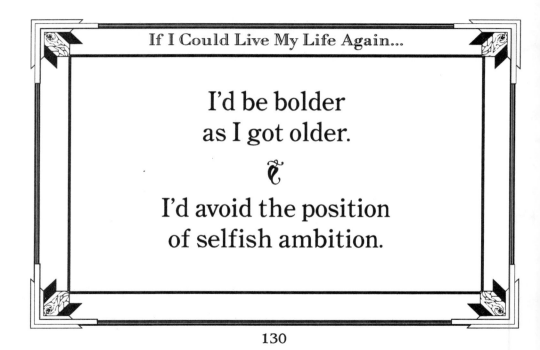

I'd avoid the position
of selfish ambition.

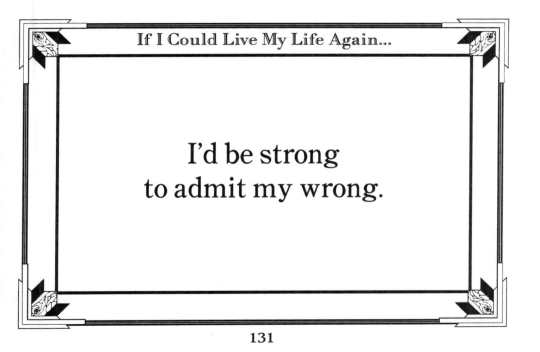

I'd be strong
to admit my wrong.

I'd build a house in winter snow
so birds would have a place to go.

℃

I'd congratulate expecting ladies
and hold more cuddly babies.

I'd play on the floor
with kids a lot more.

I'd beware of trees
with busy bumblebees.

🙖

I'd search the night sky
for a star to fly by.

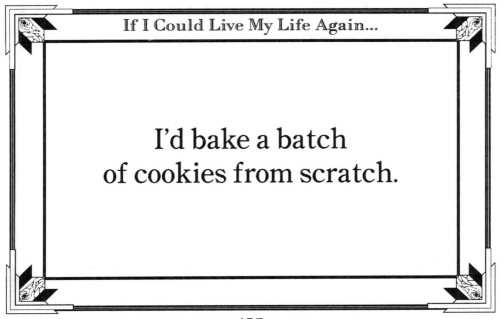

I'd bake a batch
of cookies from scratch.

I'd learn to appreciate
the guy my daughter dates.

I wouldn't huff and puff
or try to strut my stuff.

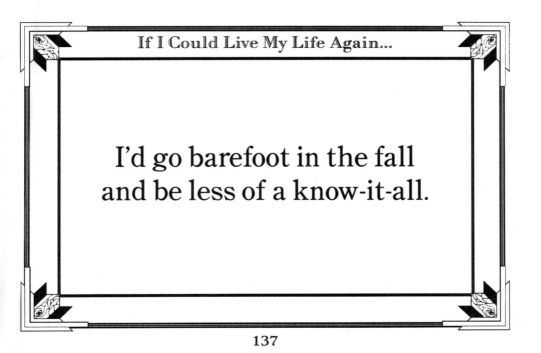

I'd go barefoot in the fall
and be less of a know-it-all.

I'd trade tickles
and pucker pickles.

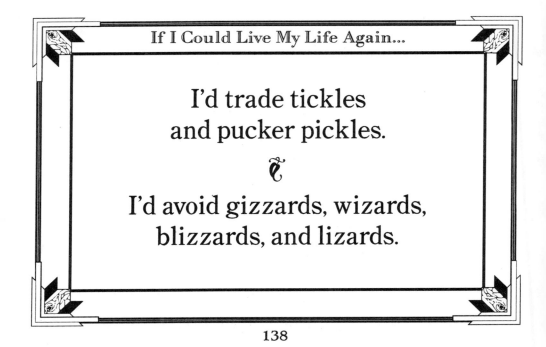

I'd avoid gizzards, wizards,
blizzards, and lizards.

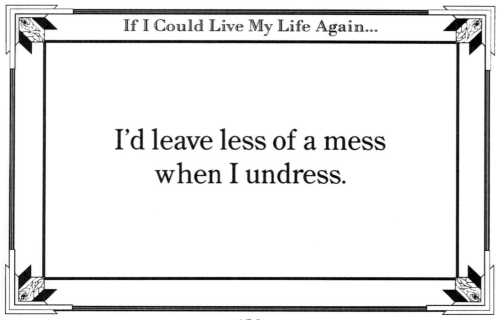

If I Could Live My Life Again...

I'd leave less of a mess
when I undress.

I'd try not to feud
when in a bad mood.

On field trips away from home,
with my kids I'd chaperon.

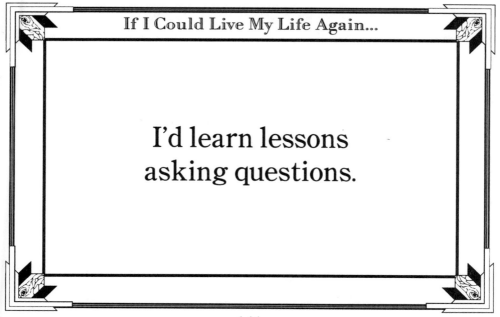

If I Could Live My Life Again...

I'd learn lessons
asking questions.

I'd try harder
to be a self-starter.

I'd consider the option
of baby adoption.

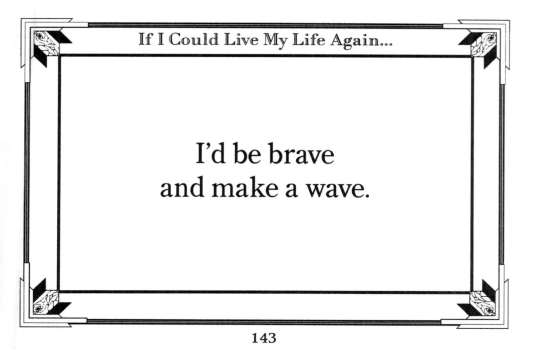

I'd be brave
and make a wave.

I'd try not to misjudge,
nor hold onto a grudge.

I'd assemble puzzle pieces
with nephews and nieces.

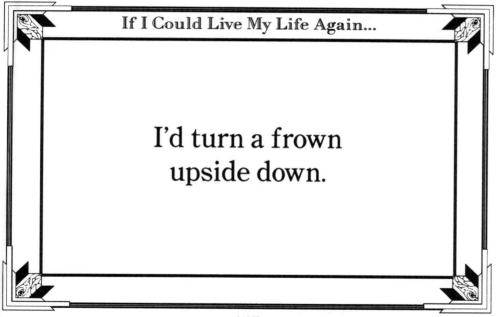

If I Could Live My Life Again...

I'd turn a frown
upside down.

I wouldn't choke
on tobacco smoke.

℃

I'd realize my pride
is often too wide.

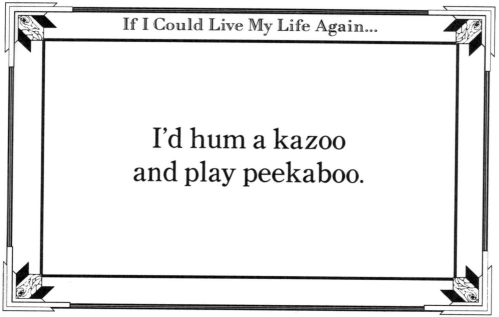

I'd hum a kazoo
and play peekaboo.

Before my bills were paid,
I'd tithe on every dollar made.

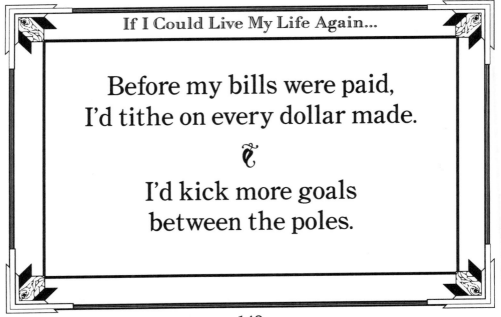

I'd kick more goals
between the poles.

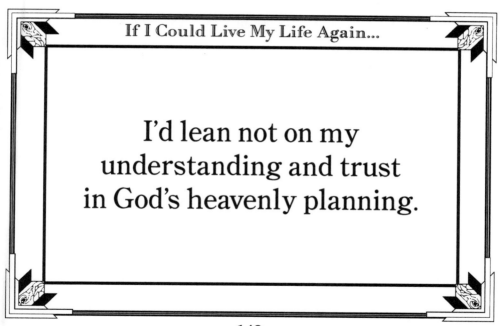

I'd lean not on my
understanding and trust
in God's heavenly planning.

I'd demonstrate integrity,
even when others couldn't see.

I'd play more make-believe
and magic-up-my-sleeve.

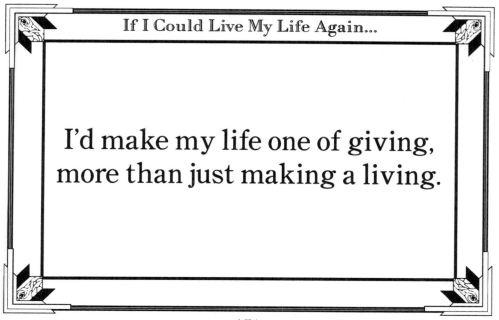

If I Could Live My Life Again...

I'd make my life one of giving,
more than just making a living.

I'd try not to overlook
balancing my checkbook.

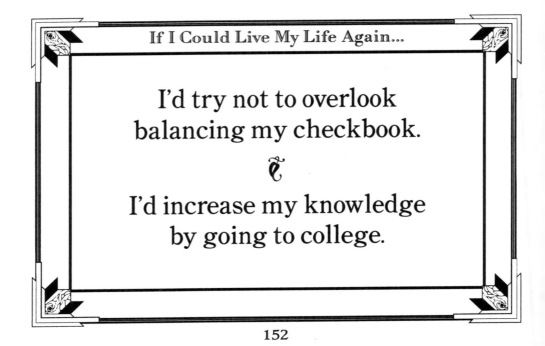

I'd increase my knowledge
by going to college.

I'd chase butterflies
under blue skies.

A TALE TO KNOW BY CYRANO

The Inspiration Behind A Legend In His Own Rhyme

Let me share with you a tale of inspiration and betrayal,
a story of poetic word, of my great, great granddad Cyrano de Berg.
For he had a tender heart and his nose was a work of art,
as a poet the part he played was that of a romantic serenade.
While another man spoke his prose, granddad hid behind his nose,
as the maiden was swayed by the rhyme of his friend's charade.
Generations later I found out about this hoax behind his snout,
and as a youth I felt betrayed by his phony masquerade.

I became ashamed of this mimicry and the heritage of my family,
but then one day I read by chance, the words he used for romance.
It was then when my heart realized the legacy of my family ties.
I saw him in a new light. My heart was touched, and now I write.
The prose composed from my pen, I propose as a new trend . . .
poetic proverbs known as *Rhymeos*™,
by the Show-It Poet™ Cyrano,
Rearranged along this path of fame, was my granddad's last name,
no longer am I called de Bergerac; I am *Cyrano De Words-u-lac*.
If you find your lines are few, the words you lack I'll choose for you.
For I've pledged to become over time . . .
a legend in my own rhyme.

WHO IS CYRANO?

a literary
dignitary
a word weaver
Rhymeo™ retriever
a prolific writer
and poetic reciter
among supermen
of the fountain pen

Cyrano De Words-u-lac
is the combined pen name of brothers
Dr. Dan the Man and Dave the Wave Davidson

PARTNERS IN RHYME
the brothers behind Cyrano's mind

More Rhymeo™ Titles
by Cyrano De Words-u-lac

Diamond Dreams
A Mother's Love Is Made Up Of . . .
Home & Heart Improvement For Men
It's Time Again To Skip A Birthday When . . .

If you have a Rhymeo™ for Cyrano
send what you've penned to the
Quill Guild ™
for Rhymeo™ Writers, Readers & Friends of Cyrano
Write or call Cyrano to receive a FREE
Quill Guild™ Rhymeo™ newsletter or for information
on the **Life Story Inventory™**, **Grand Plow Plan™**,
and **Diamond Dream** workshops.
Rhymeo Ink   P.O. Box 1416   Salem , VA 24153
CompuServe - **71175,1035**   *Prodigy* - **GCSU92A**
America Online - **rhymeo**   *E-mail* - **rhymeo@aol.com**
phone (540) 989-0592   fax (540) 989-6176
1 8 0 0   4   R H Y M E O
visit the Rhymeo™ by Cyrano web site on the Internet
http://www.rhymeo.com